FOCUS ON

PREHISTORIC LIFE

M. BENTON & E. COOK

GLOUCESTER PRESS
London . New York . Sydney

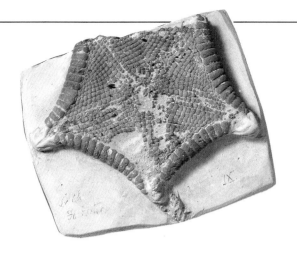

First published in
Great Britain in 1994 by
The Watts Group
96 Leonard Street
London EC2A 4RH

ISBN 0 7496 1478 1

A CIP catalogue record for this book is
available from the British Library.

Printed in Belgium

Design	David West Children's Book Design
Designer	Steve Woosnam-Savage, Flick Killerby
Series Director	Bibby Whittaker
Editor	Suzanne Melia
Picture research	Brooks Krikler Research
Illustrators	Mike Saunders
	Alex Pang
	David Burroughs

*The authors Liz Cook and Michael Benton
Phd. are based at the Dept of Geology at
Bristol University. They have both written
many books and papers on dinosaurs
and prehistoric life. They are both
involved in researching the field of
prehistory.*

INTRODUCTION

The history of life on Earth is long and complex. From the earliest forms of microscopic life, the processes of evolution have produced the great diversity of plants and animals that inhabit our Earth. Prehistory is a subject that covers a huge period of time, from the origins of life on Earth to our human ancestors. Perhaps the most dramatic and best known episode of prehistory was the reign of the dinosaurs. However, other periods were just as exciting, and in many ways more important. Each spread is colour-coded to be easily located on the timescale on page 30.

Geography
The symbol of the planet Earth shows where geographical facts and activities are included. These sections include a look at how coal deposits were formed and where coal can be found throughout the world. The pattern of the Earth's continents and the fact that they have moved is also discussed.

Language and literature
An open book is the sign for activities which involve language and literature. In these sections, information is given about the cultural and religious beliefs that exist to explain the beginnings of life on Earth. Famous novels about prehistoric life are also discussed.

Science
The microscope symbol indicates where science projects or science information is included. If the symbol is tinted green, it signals an environmental issue. How fish first managed to grow legs is discussed.

History
The sign of the scroll and hourglass shows where historical information is given. These sections look at key figures involved in the discovery of famous and important fossils and other evidence of prehistoric life.

Maths
A ruler and compass indicate maths activities. These include a look at how scientists work out if a mass extinction has occurred by counting the amount of fossils found in each layer of the Earth. How long an animal lived on the Earth can also be calculated by looking at where similar types of fossils are found how many occur in each layer of rock.

Arts, crafts and music
The symbol showing a sheet of music and art tools signals arts, crafts or musical activities. These sections look at famous films about dinosaurs and at how artists recreate prehistoric animals by looking at fossils – and how they sometimes get it wrong!

CONTENTS

ORIGINS OF LIFE

We now know that our planet was formed about 4.5 billion years ago, millions of years before any life appeared on the Earth. Many ideas have been suggested to explain how life began. About 3.5 billion years ago, the first living organisms appeared on Earth. At that time (a period called the Precambrian Age), the Earth's atmosphere contained no oxygen, the gas that animals need to breathe. The first life forms were simple, microscopic, single-celled organisms, and are known only from fossils. The oldest fossils of multi-celled animals have been found in rocks from 640 million years ago.

The age of the Earth
The scientist Lord Kelvin (1824-1907) thought that the Earth was only 100 million years old, after he calculated the amount of heat lost by the Earth since its formation. Geologists now calculate the true age of rocks by measuring their radioactive elements.

Lord Kelvin

DNA

A Bacterial Cell

Extraterrestrial life?
Most scientists think that life began on Earth through a series of chemical reactions. Energy from lightning, sunlight and volcanoes caused chemicals to react together to produce large organic molecules. A few think that comets from outer space, carrying organic chemicals, landed on the Earth's surface.

Living rocks
Stromatolites are found in some of the oldest rocks on Earth; rocks which are 3.4 billion years old. Today, living stromatolites can be seen in Shark Bay, Western Australia. Stromatolites are domes or sheets of layered limestone (3) formed by blue-green algae, which collect particles of mud (1) and cement them together (2).

1

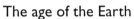

2

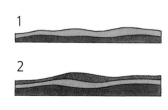

3

The Precambrian seas

In 1947, the first multi-celled fossils were found in Precambrian rocks from the Ediacara Hills in Australia. *Brachnia* was a type of jellyfish. The fossil jellyfish (below) looks similar to today's. *Dickinsonia* was a strange, worm-like organism.

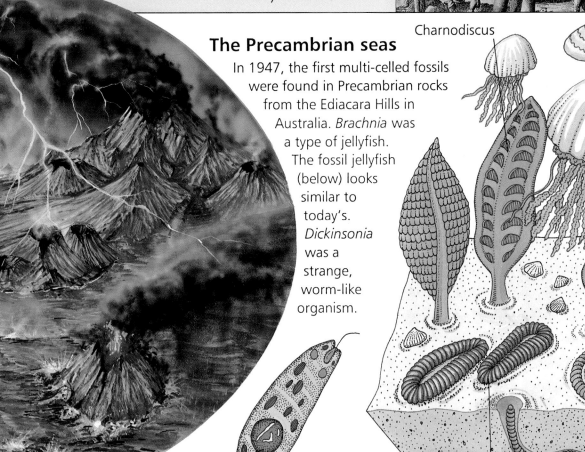

Charnodiscus

Brachnia

Nucleus

Euglena

Dickensonia

Tribrachidium

The early Earth

Shortly after the formation of the Earth, the conditions were very different from today's. Instead of an atmosphere based on oxygen, it's likely that the air was a mixture of hydrogen, methane and ammonia. The surface of the Earth was dominated by volcanoes, lava flows, and huge oceans. It is in these oceans that life began. The first life-forms were very simple single-celled organisms such as algae and bacteria. Later, more complicated living things, like the alga, *Euglena,* contained cells with a nucleus. It is the nucleus in a living cell that holds the DNA, a chemical essential for evolution.

EXPLOSION OF LIFE

During the late Precambrian Era, and the Cambrian period that followed, the diversity of invertebrates (animals without backbones) increased rapidly. It was changes in the conditions on the surface of the Earth that enabled these life-forms to evolve. Although many of these new animals, like trilobites, had hard parts in their bodies (and were easily fossilised), some had bodies made of jelly-like substances and so are rarely found today. Fossils of soft-bodied animals showing exceptional preservation were found in the Cambrian rocks of the Burgess Shale in Canada.

Arthropod respiration

Arthropods that live under water use gills to extract oxygen from the water. Those which live on land (like insects and millipedes) breathe using a system of holes, called spiracles, in their external skeleton. Air passes through the spiracles and into the muscles.

Muscle fibre

AIR

Spiracle

AIR

Opabinia, one of the rarer Burgess Shale animals. A strange-looking animal, its five compound eyes balanced on stalks and a long extension on its head was used to catch prey.

Opabinia

Trilobite

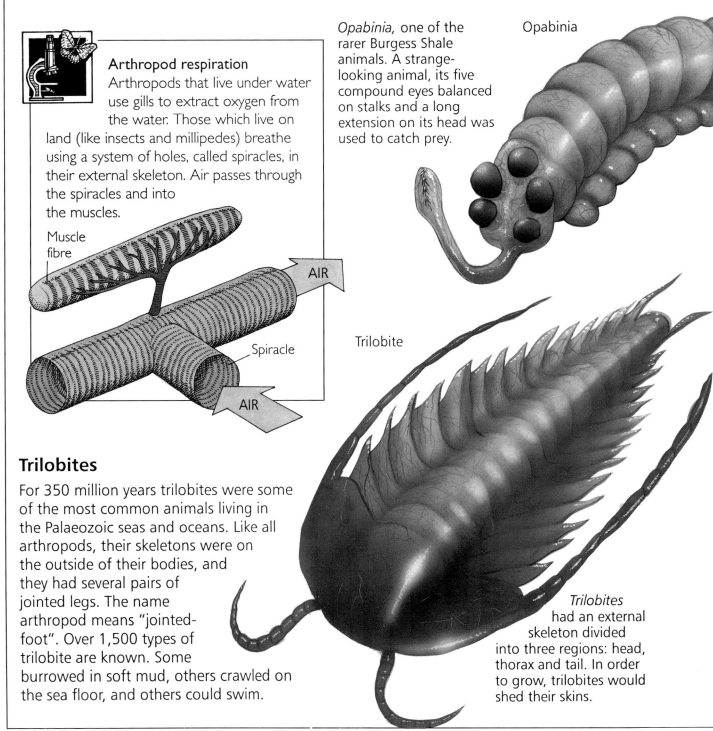

Trilobites

For 350 million years trilobites were some of the most common animals living in the Palaeozoic seas and oceans. Like all arthropods, their skeletons were on the outside of their bodies, and they had several pairs of jointed legs. The name arthropod means "jointed-foot". Over 1,500 types of trilobite are known. Some burrowed in soft mud, others crawled on the sea floor, and others could swim.

Trilobites had an external skeleton divided into three regions: head, thorax and tail. In order to grow, trilobites would shed their skins.

Odontogriphus

Odontogriphus was 6 cm long. Its mouth was surrounded by tentacles.

Marrella was a small animal, less than 2.5 cm long. Walcott called them "lace crabs".

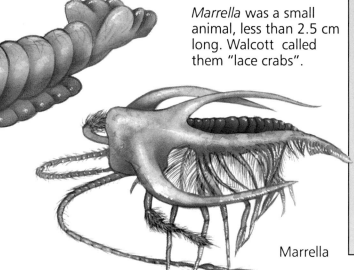

Marrella

Charles Doolittle Walcott
Charles Walcott was an American geologist who spent much of his time producing geological maps of the Canadian mountains. While collecting fossils in the mountains of British Columbia in 1910, Walcott found a slab of rock containing many interesting fossils. Today, scientists still visit the quarries explored by Walcott to collect the beautifully preserved Burgess Shale animals.

Charles Walcott

Amiskwia

The flattened, swimming animal *Amiskwia* had side and tail fins.

The Burgess Shale
The rocks of the Burgess Shale contain many animals. The animals lived in the sea and were fossilised when an underwater mud flow carried them to deeper waters. The most common animals are arthropods, including trilobites and shrimp-like creatures. It is possible that the Burgess Shale contains the first record of an animal with a notochord (a rod-like structure found in vertebrates). This animal, *Pikaia,* may be related to humans.

Upside down and back to front!
When *Hallucigenia* was first discovered and described by Simon Conway Morris, it was not known for sure which way up it should be drawn. Several years later new fossils were found. These fossils revealed that *Hallucigenia* had often been drawn upside down (right)!

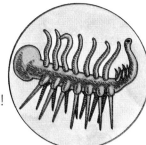

Hallucigenia

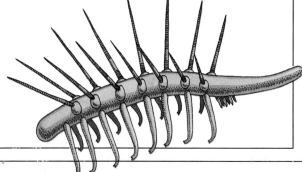

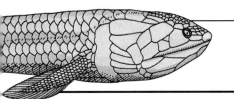

THE FIRST FISHES

The first fossil fishes are found in rocks of the Cambrian Age, but they are not well preserved. By the Ordovician, however, the fossils show enough detail for scientists to give names to the fishes. Fishes found in these rocks often had armour instead of scales and many did not have jaws. During the Devonian that followed, many new types of fishes evolved, including sharks and rays, and bony fishes. The Late Devonian also saw the evolution of *Eusthenopteron*, a fish which developed lungs and could walk on land using its strong front fins.

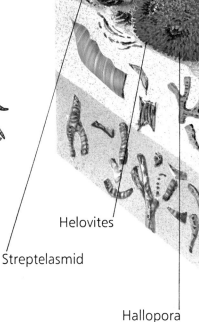

Crinoid

Rare cones

Nautiloids are molluscs and are related to ammonites. During the Ordovician, most had straight, cone-shaped shells, instead of the familiar coiled shells of ammonites. At the end of the Permian period, all the straight cones became extinct. The coiled cones survived, and evolved to produce a variety of ammonites.

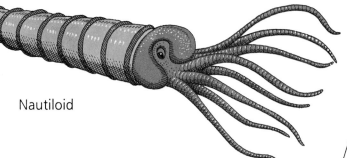

Nautiloid

Helovites

Streptelasmid

Hallopora

Protective armour
Some of the Devonian fishes were completely encased in an armour made up of bony plates, while others also relied on scales for protection. The osteostracans did not have armour that covered all of the body; it was limited to the head. The placoderms were a group of armoured fishes that evolved many strange shapes. Their heads and forequarters were covered with heavy armour. These species were not very successful and did not survive the Devonian. Some, like *Coccosteus*, were probably good swimmers. Not all Devonian fish had armour; thelodonts and anaspids were covered with small scales.

Ancient corals

Many rocks of the earlier part of the Palaeozoic contain the remains of coral reefs. Corals are first known from the Cambrian, but it was not until the Silurian that large coral reefs became common. Two types of coral built the reefs. Colonial corals (for example Favosites) are made up of many animals all living in the same stony coral. Solitary corals only have one animal living in them. The reefs were home to other creatures including crinoids, nautiloids, trilobites and fishes. Ancient corals tended to be larger than today's and lived singly, like sea anemones.

A bestseller
Hugh Miller (1802-1856) was a stonemason from Scotland. He collected many important fossils from the Old Red Sandstone which outcrops in northern Scotland. Many were of Devonian, armoured, jawless fish. Miller is famous for a series of popular geology books he wrote in the 1840s and 1850s. These books were bestsellers at the time.

Alive and kicking
Coelacanths are known from fossils in rocks ranging from the Devonian to the Cretaceous, when it was thought they became extinct. In 1938, a strange fish was caught by fishermen off the south-eastern coast of Africa. Scientists noticed the similarity between this fish with its leg-like fins (called *Latimeria*), and fossils of prehistoric fish, and decided that the coelacanths are still alive today! *Latimeria* lives in the deep waters of the Indian Ocean.

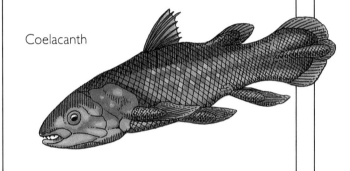

Coelacanth

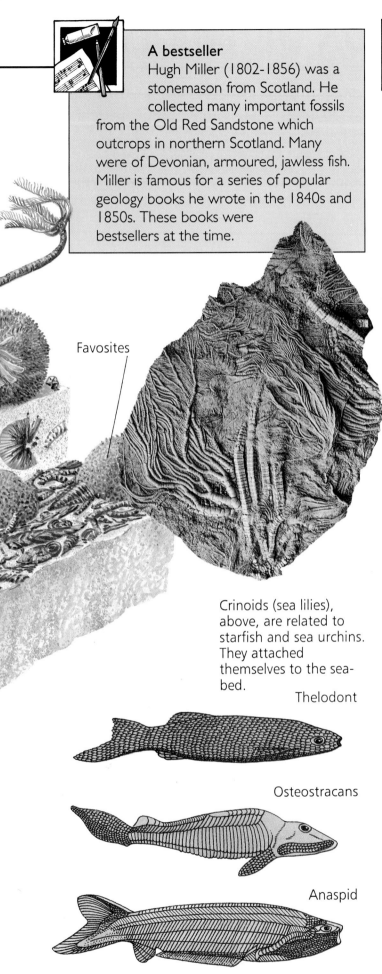

Favosites

Crinoids (sea lilies), above, are related to starfish and sea urchins. They attached themselves to the sea-bed.

Jawless fish
Most of the earliest fish did not have jaws. They belong to class Agnatha, which means "no jaws". They had a simple hole for a mouth and many must have grubbed about for organic debris in the sediment under the water. Today, there are two living groups of agnathans, the lampreys and the hagfish. It is thought that the class Gnathostomata (all of the vertebrates with jaws) evolved from jawless fish. The jaws were formed from some of the bones that supported the gills.

Thelodont

Osteostracans

Anaspid

Dinithys

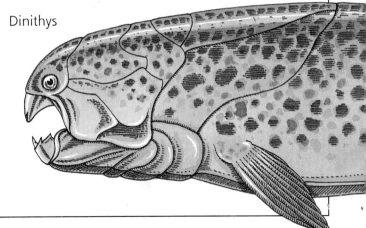

INVASION OF THE LAND

Life on land probably began during the Silurian period when plants and arthropods evolved the ability to live in air. Some people believe vertebrates (animals with backbones) moved onto dry land when their ponds and lakes dried out. In fact, it's more likely that they wanted the better selection of plants and animals found there. This meant they had to change their breathing mechanisms, adapt to new kinds of food and develop new ways of moving. The first terrestrial (land-living) vertebrates were the amphibians, able to live on land and water.

Lobefinned fish

The lobefins were common during the Devonian period, and their fossils are especially common in the Old Red Sandstone. They are all bony fishes and have paired, muscular fins which they could use when moving about on land. Lobefins, like *Osteolepis,* ate the vegetation that grew around the ponds they lived in. Others, such as *Glyptolepis,* were predators. Lobefins are important because they were the ancestors of the amphibians, the first land-living vertebrates.

Lobefinned fish

Fins to feet

For vertebrates to be able to move around on land, the bones in their limbs had to change. Lobefinned fishes, like *Eusthenopteron,* had fins to move along, but with all the bones needed to act like a leg (below left). The bones that make up the limbs of early amphibians, like *Eryops* (below right), show similarities.

Eusthenopteron

Eryops

Onto the shore

The first fossil of a terrestrial vertebrate is called *Ichthyostega.* Specimens were found in Greenland. This 1-metre-long animal lived during the Late Devonian. Its legs were strong enough for it to walk about slowly on land, but its large tail suggests that it spent a lot of time in water like *Eogyrinus* (below).

Ichthyostega

Eogyrinus

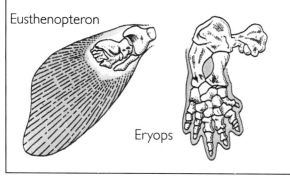

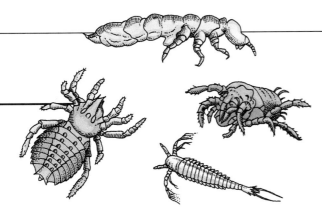

Creeping and crawling

Some of the first animals to make the giant step from water onto land were the invertebrate arthropods. These jointed animals had lived in the sea, and emerged onto land to evolve into spiders, insects and millipedes. They fed on the simple plants that had begun to grow.

Zdenek Burian

The Czech artist Zdenek Burian is probably best known for his illustrations for the book *Life Before Man*. His reconstructions cover the history of life on Earth, from earliest times right up to the last Ice Age. During his career, from the 1940s to 1960s, Burian painted hundreds of prehistoric scenes, and these can still be seen in many books today.

Mudskippers (above) live in tropical estuaries and mangrove swamps. These bony fish have stiffly-rayed pectoral fins that are used to prop themselves up. This enables them to move on land in the same way as the first fishes moved out of their ponds. They use their swim bladder and their gills to take in oxygen, gulping in air at the surface.

Eat your greens

Plant fossils do not become common until the Silurian. Fossils found in the Rhynie Chert in northern Scotland tell scientists about the plants and animals living in the Early Devonian swamps. The chert (a flinty rock) preserves the plants so well that some of them show the damage caused by the hungry arthropods who chomped on them!

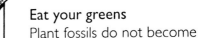

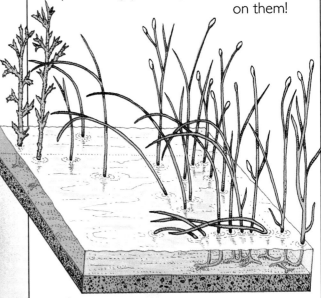

THE COAL SWAMPS

During the Carboniferous, the surface of the Earth was dominated by large expanses of tropical forest. These forests contained giant lycopod ferns, over 40 metres tall, club mosses and giant horsetails. The tropical swamps were home to many kinds of large amphibians (vertebrates that need to return to water to lay their eggs). Over millions of years, dead plant material was slowly fossilised to produce coal, a carbon-rich rock.

Mazon Creek fossils

The rocks containing the Mazon Creek creatures are recovered from the spoil heaps produced by coal mining. These fossils are an example of exceptional preservation of invertebrates. Some of the plants and animals lived in the sea, like those illustrated here. Others would have lived in freshwater streams and ponds. The fossils are found in nodules (rounded lumps) of ironstone, a rock which is rich in iron and preserves soft parts of animals. These include worms, jellyfish, insects, scorpions and spiders.

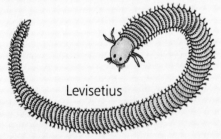

Levisetius

Octomedusa   Pterochiton

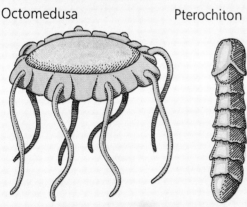

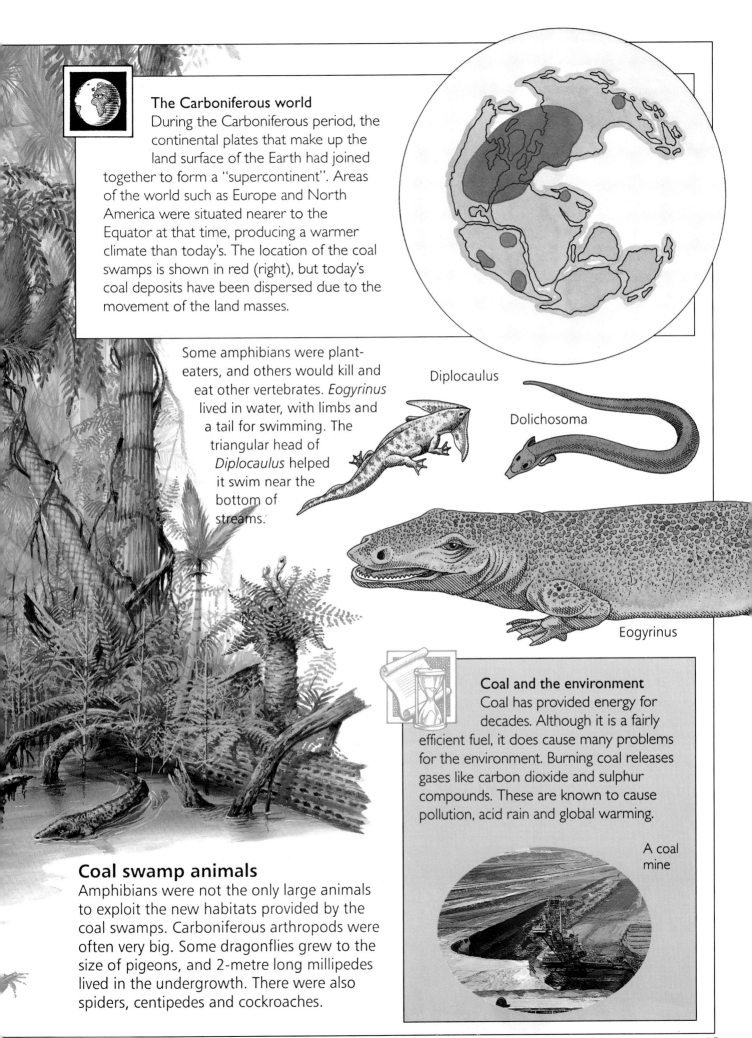

The Carboniferous world

During the Carboniferous period, the continental plates that make up the land surface of the Earth had joined together to form a "supercontinent". Areas of the world such as Europe and North America were situated nearer to the Equator at that time, producing a warmer climate than today's. The location of the coal swamps is shown in red (right), but today's coal deposits have been dispersed due to the movement of the land masses.

Some amphibians were plant-eaters, and others would kill and eat other vertebrates. *Eogyrinus* lived in water, with limbs and a tail for swimming. The triangular head of *Diplocaulus* helped it swim near the bottom of streams.

Diplocaulus

Dolichosoma

Eogyrinus

Coal and the environment

Coal has provided energy for decades. Although it is a fairly efficient fuel, it does cause many problems for the environment. Burning coal releases gases like carbon dioxide and sulphur compounds. These are known to cause pollution, acid rain and global warming.

A coal mine

Coal swamp animals

Amphibians were not the only large animals to exploit the new habitats provided by the coal swamps. Carboniferous arthropods were often very big. Some dragonflies grew to the size of pigeons, and 2-metre long millipedes lived in the undergrowth. There were also spiders, centipedes and cockroaches.

THE SAILBACKS

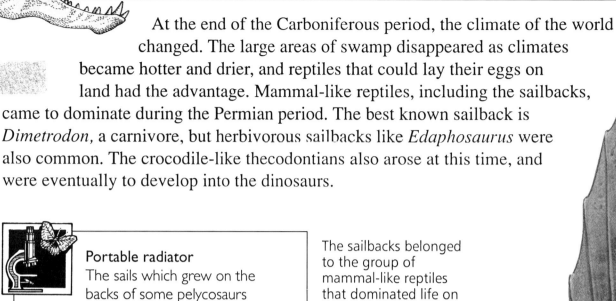

At the end of the Carboniferous period, the climate of the world changed. The large areas of swamp disappeared as climates became hotter and drier, and reptiles that could lay their eggs on land had the advantage. Mammal-like reptiles, including the sailbacks, came to dominate during the Permian period. The best known sailback is *Dimetrodon*, a carnivore, but herbivorous sailbacks like *Edaphosaurus* were also common. The crocodile-like thecodontians also arose at this time, and were eventually to develop into the dinosaurs.

Portable radiator

The sails which grew on the backs of some pelycosaurs (sailbacks) were strange structures made of elongated vertebral spines. Vertebrae are the bones that make up an animal's backbone. These spines were covered in a layer of skin rich in blood vessels. The sail was used to keep the animal's body at the right temperature whatever the outside temperature. In order to warm up, the sailback stood with the sail sideways to the sun (below). To cool down, it faced the sun (right), allowing as few sun rays as possible to touch the surface of its body.

Sun

Sun rays

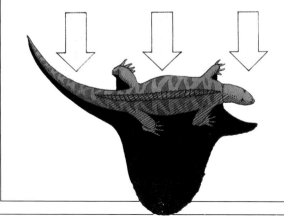

The sailbacks belonged to the group of mammal-like reptiles that dominated life on land during the Permian period. The smallest fed on insects and worms, the larger ones preyed on the smallest, and the largest of all fed on all of the others. Flesh-eaters dominated the continents, though a few plant-eating forms began to evolve in Russia, and these gradually became the most common.

Dimetrodon

Dimetrodon

From the Early Permian of Texas, New Mexico and Oklahoma, Dimetrodon had a large sail and grew to about 3 metres. Apart from its use in temperature control, it has been suggested that Dimetrodon's sail was used in pre-mating displays or for camouflage.

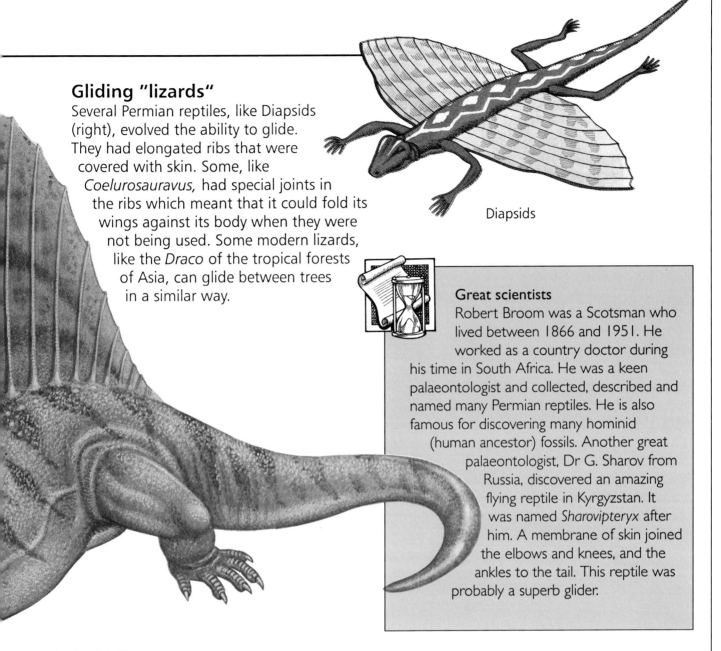

Gliding "lizards"

Several Permian reptiles, like Diapsids (right), evolved the ability to glide. They had elongated ribs that were covered with skin. Some, like *Coelurosauravus,* had special joints in the ribs which meant that it could fold its wings against its body when they were not being used. Some modern lizards, like the *Draco* of the tropical forests of Asia, can glide between trees in a similar way.

Diapsids

Great scientists

Robert Broom was a Scotsman who lived between 1866 and 1951. He worked as a country doctor during his time in South Africa. He was a keen palaeontologist and collected, described and named many Permian reptiles. He is also famous for discovering many hominid (human ancestor) fossils. Another great palaeontologist, Dr G. Sharov from Russia, discovered an amazing flying reptile in Kyrgyzstan. It was named *Sharovipteryx* after him. A membrane of skin joined the elbows and knees, and the ankles to the tail. This reptile was probably a superb glider.

Moving continents

The pattern of continents on the Earth's surface is constantly changing. In 1915, a German scientist called Alfred Wegener popularised the theory of continental drift. The evidence he used came from the shape of the continents (they fit together) and the presence of fossils such as this leaf of a seed fern, *Glossopteris*. This plant is associated with rocks of the Southern hemisphere, but is spread throughout the separate land masses. The continents actually "float" on the Earth's mantle (layer of molten rock) and move around very slowly on the currents.

Glossopteris

THE GREATEST EXTINCTION

Mass extinctions (when many species die out at the same time) have occurred throughout the history of life on Earth. Although the most dramatic and well-known extinction event was the one that destroyed the dinosaurs, this was in fact quite small compared to the great Permian-Triassic extinction. At the end of the Permian period, 73 per cent of the vertebrate families on Earth disappeared. Half of the world's marine invertebrates were also destroyed. Many theories have been suggested to account for this event, but scientists don't really know what happened as not many clues were left behind.

Periodic extinctions

When the American scientists, Raup and Sepkoski, looked at the various extinction events experienced by the Earth, they noticed a peak in the extinction rate approximately every 26 million years. Although this could be coincidence, they decided to look for an explanation for it. They decided that nothing on Earth could possibly produce such a pattern, so they looked to space. The resulting theory is that every 26 million years or so our planet moves through a cloud of asteroids (small planets that move around the Sun), some of which hit the Earth with disastrous effects on animal and plant life.

At the end of the Permian, many reptiles had become more like mammals, and just as it seemed that the age of the mammals was about to dawn, mammal-like reptiles including the dog-like *Cynognathus*, above, suddenly went into decline. They had dominated the continents for 70 million years.

An extinction event?

Ever since life on Earth began, the process of extinction has operated. Small numbers of species suffer extinction all the time. This is called the "background extinction rate". Scientists calculate the presence of an extinction event by looking at the types and amounts of fossils in different layers of rock. The length of time an organism has been on Earth, from its first to last appearances, is known as its "range". If scientists notice that many types of animal or plant are disappearing at the same time, they call this a "mass extinction". Many of the boundaries between the geological time periods are marked by the occurrence of a mass extinction.

Some major groups of animals, such as trilobites, left, completely died out during the Permian. Fossil trilobites are only found in rocks older than the Permian period.

John Phillips

In 1841, John Phillips replaced the old method of dividing up geological time with a method that is now familiar to all earth scientists working today. Previously, the history of the Earth had been classified as primary, transitional, secondary and alluvial. Phillips' system divided time into Palaeozoic (ancient-life), Mesozoic (middle life) and Caenozoic (new life).

John Phillips

Causes of extinction

Before the evolution of humans, extinction events were caused by processes such as changes in climate, competition between species and the impact of extraterrestrial objects. Throughout our short history, humans have caused the destruction of many animals and plants. The classic example of this is the loss of the dodo due to hunting by sailors. Today, many species of animals (like the blue whale below) and plants are at risk, either from too much hunting or through loss of their natural habitats.

One class of echinoderms, the crinoids or sea-lilies, were fixed to the floor of the ocean by roots. This crinoid, *Taxocrinus,* is from Dudley, England.

This fossilised amphibian (below) from the Permian period was found in Pfalz in Germany.

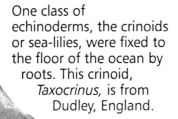

Saltoposuchus evolved after the Permian extinction. It is typical of the crocodile-like animals from which the dinosaurs evolved.

Saltoposuchus

DINOSAURS

Dinosaurs are probably the best-known form of prehistoric life. They ruled the Earth from the Late Triassic until the end of the Cretaceous, a total of 165 million years. Although we usually think of dinosaurs as one group (or order) of animal, two distinct types existed. The first were the saurischian, or lizard-hipped dinosaurs. Saurischian dinosaurs included the theropods (meat-eaters) and the giant sauropods (plant-eaters). The second group were the ornithischians, or bird-hipped dinosaurs. Most plant-eating dinosaurs were ornithischians.

The first dinosaurs
In 1842, Sir Richard Owen recognised that some large bones found years before were different from living reptiles and he grouped them together as the "Dinosauria". The first creature to be described was *Megalosaurus*, a large carnivorous dinosaur found in the Jurassic rocks of the Cotswolds in England. Two others were herbivores, and of Cretaceous age. *Hylaeosaurus* was an armoured dinosaur.

The Jurassic world
By the Jurassic, dinosaurs ruled the Earth. During the Early Jurassic, the most common dinosaurs were the prosauropods, ancestors of the sauropods (reptile feet); small ornithischians, for example, the fabrosaurs; and the carnivorous *Megalosaurus*. By the Middle Jurassic, the giant sauropods, like *Cetiosaurus and Brachiosaurus,* came into their own. Other herbivores included stegosaurs (plated reptiles), and a selection of ornithopods (bird feet). These animals were hunted by *Megalosaurus* and *Ornithomimius*.

Jurassic

The Triassic world
The Triassic world was dominated by many groups of large vertebrates including rhynchosaurs and thecodontians. Dinosaurs evolved from the thecodontians, and first appeared in great numbers during the Late Triassic.

Masrocnemus

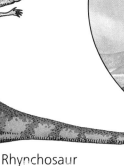

Rhynchosaur

Triassic

Dinostars
One of the most successful dinosaur films is Steven Spielberg's *Jurassic Park* (right). Based on the book of the same name by Michael Crichton. Jurassic Park is a dinosaur theme park created by a businessman. But things go horribly wrong! The dinosaurs were brought to life for the movie by computer graphics and model animation. It's probably the most realistic dinosaur film ever!

Cretaceous

We know from fossils that many dinosaurs laid eggs. Some fossil eggs (below) have been found containing babies.

Cretaceous world
At the end of the Cretaceous, the reign of the dinosaurs ended. This may have been caused by a meteorite hitting the Earth. Evidence for this comes from the iridium layer (marked by the white circle below) which is a rare element found at the Cretaceous-Tertiary boundary. Other theories suggest dinosaurs died out slowly due to a change in climate.

Iridium layer

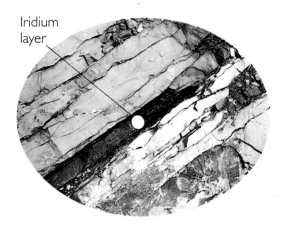

Hot blooded or not?
Dinosaurs used to be thought of as large, slow, stupid reptiles. But today, even though scientists think they led more active lives, the question of their metabolism (how their bodies produced heat) has still not been decided. Some people think that dinosaurs were warm-blooded, like mammals, generating their own body heat without having to use the Sun's rays to warm them up. However, most scientists agree that the large size of their bodies probably meant that a dinosaur stayed warm, even though it could not produce heat internally. This meant they could act in an almost "warm-blooded" manner.

THE FLYING REPTILES

The oldest pterosaurs are found in rocks from the Late Triassic. Pterosaurs were the first vertebrates to develop true, active flight, although gliding reptiles are known from the Permian. The earliest fossil bird is called *Archaeopteryx,* which means "ancient wing". Pterosaurs evolved a wide variety of shapes and sizes; the largest, *Quetzalcoatlus*, had a wing span of 12 metres, the largest flying animal ever.

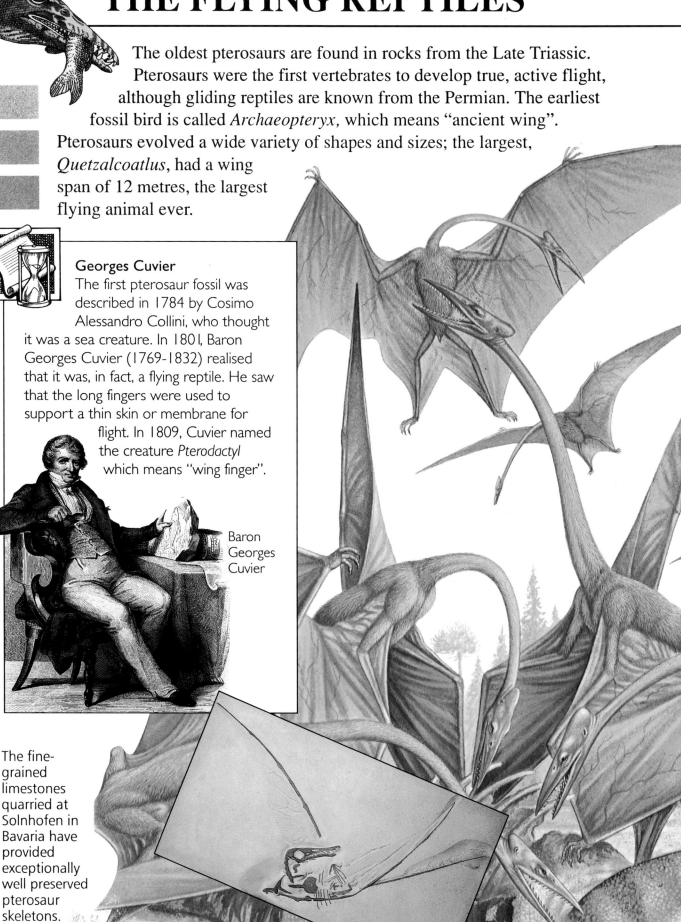

Georges Cuvier
The first pterosaur fossil was described in 1784 by Cosimo Alessandro Collini, who thought it was a sea creature. In 1801, Baron Georges Cuvier (1769-1832) realised that it was, in fact, a flying reptile. He saw that the long fingers were used to support a thin skin or membrane for flight. In 1809, Cuvier named the creature *Pterodactyl* which means "wing finger".

Baron Georges Cuvier

The fine-grained limestones quarried at Solnhofen in Bavaria have provided exceptionally well preserved pterosaur skeletons.

In order to prevent all the different species of Pterosaurs from competing for food, they evolved many different skull designs. These three species either ate different kinds of fish, or they caught their fish in different ways.

Dzungaripterus

Dimorphodon

Tropeognathus

A trick of the tail

Two types of pterosaur existed. Rhamphorhynchoids all had long tails, used to improve the efficiency of flight. *Sordes pilosus* (hairy evil spirit) was a very small rhamphorhynchoid. The first short-tailed pterosaur, or *pterodactyl,* appeared in the Upper Jurassic. Throughout the Cretaceous, the *pterodactyls* evolved many weird and wonderful shapes.

Origins of dragons

Folk tales from all over the world tell us of dragons and other flying monsters. In all of the legends, dragons are seen as being massive, flying reptiles. It would be nice to think that fossil pterosaur bones were responsible for starting these stories. Unfortunately, legends of dragons have been around for thousands of years, while pterosaurs are quite new to science.

Dragon

Lost Worlds

It's not just the ancient story tellers who were fascinated by flying monsters. Sir Arthur Conan Doyle (1859-1930), a Victorian author, had the heroes of his book *The Lost World* meeting pterosaurs on a mountain plateau in South America. The plateau was populated by all manner of supposedly long-dead creatures from the age of the dinosaurs.

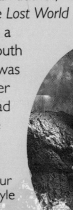

Arthur Conan Doyle

THE MESOZOIC OCEANS

During the Mesozoic Era (which includes the Triassic, the Jurassic and the Cretaceous periods) the world's oceans were home to many large marine reptiles. Some of these creatures are familiar to us today, like the crocodiles and turtles. Others, like *Ichthyosaurus* (fish lizard) look similar to dolphins, but were reptiles not mammals. Marine reptiles were a very important part of the Mesozoic oceans, but they were not the only creatures to live in them. Some of the most familiar and plentiful fossils, such as the ammonites and "Devil's Toenail" lived in the seas at that time.

Snake stones

Ammonites were molluscs (animals with a shell), distantly related to snails and shellfish. They floated in the water, catching food with their tentacles. When people first found these coiled fossils, they thought that they were snakes which had been turned to stone.

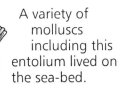

A variety of molluscs including this entolium lived on the sea-bed.

Entolium

Ammonite

Plesiosaurs had long necks that they used to snatch small fish from the water.

Plesiosaurs

Layers of history

An age can be given to the rocks by looking at the fossils they contain, or by comparing sequences of layers of rock. The layers of rock are called strata. They were originally all more or less level, but movements of the Earth's crust have caused them to move about, sinking and rising.

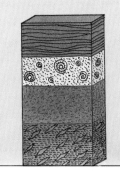

The chalk seas

During the Upper Cretaceous, the world's oceans contained micro-organisms which are now preserved as chalk rock. They lived in the surface of the sea, and when they died, their bodies sank to the sea-bed, forming chalk.

Ichthyosaur

Ichthyosaurs were dolphin-like reptiles that grew up to 16 metres in length.

Pliosaurs had very short necks, and skulls more adapted to kill larger animals, possibly even ichthyosaurs and plesiosaurs.

Pliosaur

Child scientist
In 1810, Mary Anning found her first whole ichthyosaur fossil at Lyme Regis in England (below). She was only eleven years old at the time. During her life, Mary Anning found many specimens, some of which she sold to British scientists. You may have heard the rhyme "She sells sea shells on the sea shore" which was possibly written about her.

Lyme Regis

Sea dragons
Since the discovery of their fossils, many attempts to produce reconstructions of marine reptiles have been made. Most of the earlier drawings (below) show seas full of fish, ammonites and reptiles all in dramatic poses, or looking like the Loch Ness Monster, not at all like the modern graceful images of them.

EARLY MAMMALS

Mammals evolved from a group of reptiles that existed long before the dinosaurs. Throughout the Triassic, certain carnivorous reptiles, the cynodonts, grew to resemble mammals. These mammal-like reptiles were fairly small, about the size of a dog. The first true mammals were small shrew-like beasts, such as *Megazostrodon* (below). It was probably covered with hair and was "warm-blooded". Today, mammals can be divided into three groups: the monotremes, marsupials, and placental mammals.

Megazostrodon

Barylambda lived in the Early Tertiary.

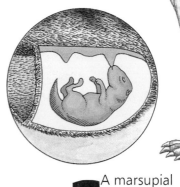

What is a mammal?

Mammals are "warm-blooded" animals covered in hair. They are able to produce heat inside their bodies. Most give birth to live young, although the monotremes lay eggs. All feed their young milk. Some mammals look after their young in special pouches. Such animals are called marsupials, and include the kangaroos and wallabies. Mammals have adapted to live on land, in the sea (for example seals, dolphins and whales) and in the air (for example bats).

A marsupial protects and feeds its underdeveloped embryo in a pouch.

William Buckland

Causing a sensation

William Buckland (1784-1856) worked as Professor of Geology at Oxford University and as the Dean of Westminster in London. He was an eccentric character who kept many strange pets, including a bear and a jackal. He is most famous for describing the carnivorous dinosaur *Megalosaurus*. He also described the first Jurassic mammal, *Amphitherium*. His announcement that mammals had lived at the time of great reptiles caused a great sensation at the time!

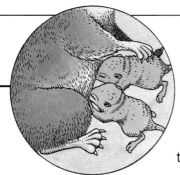

Placental mammals (such as humans and rodents) feed their unborn young through a placenta. They produce milk to feed their young after they are born.

Mammalian evolution

From the Triassic period until the end of the Cretaceous, 155 million years later, mammals were very small, never growing larger than a cat. At the start of the Tertiary period, they evolved very quickly and filled many of the niches left by the dinosaurs. Today, mammals are found on every continent and have even travelled to the Moon!

Meniscotherium

Lions

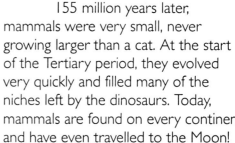

Monotremes are mammals that lay eggs. Their oldest fossils are known from Early Cretaceous rocks. Today, monotremes like the spiny ant-eater and duck-billed platypus, live in Australia.

Mammals vs dinosaurs

Mammals and dinosaurs shared the Earth for 155 million years. For many years, it was thought the mammals were responsible for the extinction of the dinosaurs. Scientists described the dinosaurs of the Cretaceous as slow and stupid, claiming they were not able to compete with the active and intelligent mammals. We now know that mammals did not kill off the dinosaurs, even though they would have eaten dinosaur eggs given the chance!

Echidnas resemble large hedgehogs.

Ealiest mammals

The earliest known true mammals, from the end of the Triassic 190 million years ago, were found in South Wales, China, North America, and Southern Africa. During the age of dinosaurs, they hunted at night and many of their rodent descendants are still nocturnal.

Planetetherium

THE GRASSLANDS

During the Palaeocene and Eocene, the numbers of mammalian species increased very quickly as they evolved to make the most of their changing environment. This process is called an "adaptive radiation". All of the ancestors of today's mammal groups, including whales, bats, horses, monkeys and apes appeared at this time. Examples of the best preserved mammals come from the oil shales at Messel in Germany. The fossils are so well preserved that the fur and even some partly digested food can be identified.

The "dawn horse"

American fossil collector, Othniel Marsh, decided that the earliest horse ancestor would be found in America. He even named this animal *Eohippus*, which means "dawn horse". Marsh did find fossils of primitive horses, but they were the same as the European early horse *Hyracotherium* already found by British scientist Thomas Huxley.

Huxley   Marsh

The hunted

Herds of gazelles, large elephants, for example *Deinotherium*, and *Moropus*, a bizarre ungulate (hoofed mammal), lived in the grasslands and forests of the north.

Deinotherium

Moropus

Gazelles

Early hyena

Biting cat

Early dog

Sabre-toothed tiger

The hunters

During the Oligocene, carnivorous mammals split into two groups, the cat-like feliforms and the dog-like caniforms. One group of early cats developed teeth that grew to a massive size. These were the sabre-toothed cats. The sabre-tooths included *Eusmilus* and the biting cat *Nimravus*.

Horse evolution

The earliest horse, called *Hyracotherium*, was only the size of a small dog. Through their history, horses have become larger, their legs have increased in length and the number of toes on their feet has been reduced.
As they evolved to exploit the grasslands, horses lost toes and acquired deeper teeth for chewing tougher grasses.

Equus
one toe

Pliohippus
one toe

Merychippus
lateral toes

Mesohippus
three toes

Hyracotherium
four toes

Little and large

Although the grassland mammals grew to massive size, they were tiny compared to the dinosaurs. For example, *Indricotherium*, which lived during the Oligocene, was up to 5.4 metres tall, and is the largest mammal to have walked on Earth. However, the sauropod dinosaurs were much larger. *Brachiosaurus* was 25 metres long, 15 metres tall, and may have weighed 50 tonnes. The largest animal of all time is the blue whale (a marine mammal) which reaches lengths of 30 metres.

Trilophodon

Charles Knight

Charles Knight, an American artist, was one of the first people to bring prehistoric animals to life. He produced many excellent colour paintings and models which are still used by the American museums. Knight painted dinosaurs, like *Laelaps*, in realistic and lively positions. He helped to reject the old idea of slow, elephantine dinosaurs and paved the way for more sprightly images of dinosaurs.

Knight

Proconsul (right) was one of the earliest apes from Kenya. Scientists think that *Proconsul* ate plant material, especially fruit. Fossils of *Proconsul* have been found with certain plant fossils that suggest that it lived in areas of forest and grassland.

27

THE ORIGINS OF HUMANS

The history of humans and our direct ancestors goes back some four million years. Our earliest ancestors evolved in the African savannas (grasslands). From here, the early humans spread out and colonised Europe and Asia, and eventually the whole world. There have been many steps along the evolutionary line leading to the modern species of human, *Homo sapiens*, which means "wise man". Some human ancestors have names that reflect their way of life; for example *Homo habilis* means "handy man", so called because the first stone tools were found with these human fossils.

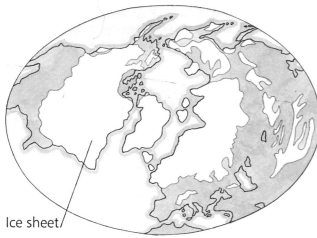

Ice sheet

Life in the Ice Age

As the climate grew cooler, huge lumbering mammoths, woolly rhinoceroses and herds of bison roamed the frozen land. Their thick, shaggy coats helped them to adapt to the cold. Early people at this time settled in the warmer regions of the world.

Woolly Rhinoceros

Bison

Wolves

The Earth has been experiencing periodic ice ages for many millions of years. Ice ages, also known as glacials, are separated by warmer time periods called interglacials. The most recent ice age occurred during the Pleistocene. The map above shows the furthest extent of the ice sheets during the last ice age.

Sculpting the Earth

Glaciers (right) push soil and rocks ahead of them like giant bulldozers, leaving behind steep valleys, deep lakes and high, craggy mountains. Most glaciers flow extremely slowly, moving less than 30 centimetres per day. The effects of ice movement during the Ice Age can be seen in large parts of Europe and North America.

Mammoths in the freezer

Frozen mammoths are occasionally found preserved in the permafrost of northern Russia. These animals died more than 10,000 years ago. After death they were covered over, often by small landslides, and have remained frozen ever since.

Woolly Mammoth

In 1973, an American palaeontologist, Don Johanson, while fossil hunting in East Africa, found the oldest human ancestor. The fossils are from a female who could walk upright in the same manner as modern humans. The specimen was named *Australopithecus afarensis,* although she is often called by her nickname "Lucy". She is between 1 and 1.2 metres tall, with a brain size of only 400cm³ and an ape-like face.

Our ancestors

Although we are not directly related, humans and living apes share a common ancestor in *Ramapithecus.* The first humans appeared between 3 and 4 million years ago and belong to the genus *Australopithecus.* Between 1.6 million and 200,000 years ago, our ancestors moved out of Africa and into Europe. The humans most people think of as "cavemen", the *Neanderthals,* populated much of Europe. They were replaced by *Homo sapiens,* about 30,000 years ago.

Ramapithecus

Neanderthal

Tar pit fossils

The Rancho La Brea tar pits of Los Angeles have produced thousands of beautifully preserved skeletons from animals that lived there millions of years ago and got stuck in the pits. Animals found in the tar include elephants, giant ground sloths, wolves, sabre-toothed tigers and birds.

Timescale

Geological time is measured in hundreds of millions of years. To make it more simple, geologists divide up the Earth's history into sections called eras, and these are then divided into periods, based on the kinds of creatures that lived at the time. The first 4,000 million years of the Earth's history is called the Precambrian Era and very few fossils have been found from this time. The next era, the Paleozoic Era, charts the development of life from sea-living organisms to the complex creatures that lived on the land. The third era, the Mesozoic Era, was the time of the dinosaurs and other giant reptiles. In the last 65 million years, the Cenozoic Era, the mammals began to dominate the Earth, bringing us to the present day and man's domination.

mya = million years ago

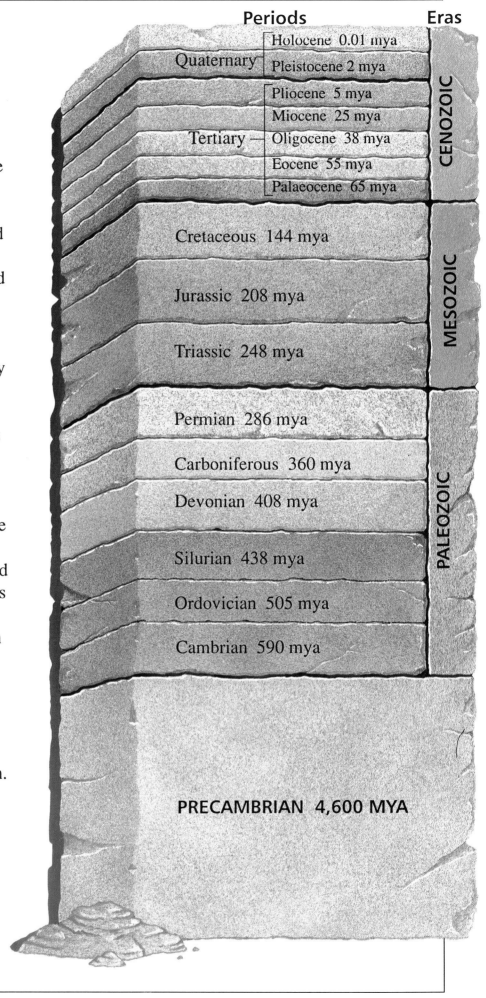

Periods

Eras

Quaternary	Holocene 0.01 mya	
	Pleistocene 2 mya	CENOZOIC
Tertiary	Pliocene 5 mya	
	Miocene 25 mya	
	Oligocene 38 mya	
	Eocene 55 mya	
	Palaeocene 65 mya	
Cretaceous 144 mya		
Jurassic 208 mya		MESOZOIC
Triassic 248 mya		
Permian 286 mya		
Carboniferous 360 mya		
Devonian 408 mya		
Silurian 438 mya		PALEOZOIC
Ordovician 505 mya		
Cambrian 590 mya		

PRECAMBRIAN 4,600 MYA

GLOSSARY

Algae Group of plants that includes seaweeds and many pondweeds, as well as many single-celled plants.

Amphibians Backboned animals that live on dry land, but must return to the water to breed.

Aquatic Living for much, if not all of the time in the water.

Arthropod A group of animals with jointed legs. Includes insects, spiders and crustaceans.

Bacterium Extremely small, one-celled creature with a very simple nucleus.

Carnivore An animal that feeds on other animals.

Continental drift Change in the layout of the Earth's surface by movement of the plates that support the lands and oceans.

DNA Abbreviation for deoxyribose nucleic acid, the chemical in all living things that codes information to control their development.

Era An interval of geological time, comprising several periods.

Extinction The disappearance, or dying out, of a species or other group.

Fossil The remains of a plant or animal that once lived, usually preserved in rock.

Geology The study of the Earth, its history and the processes that shape it.

Habitat The surroundings in which a plant or animal lives, including plant life, other animals, physical landscape and climate.

Herbivore An animal that eats plants.

Invertebrate Animal without a spine or backbone.

Mammal-like reptiles The large group of reptiles that were important in the 100 million years before the dinosaurs. Includes the ancestors of the mammals.

Mammals Hairy, backboned animals which are warm-blooded and feed their young on millk.

Marsupial A class of primitive mammals who give birth to under-developed young and raise them in a pouch.

Monotremes Primitive mammals that lay eggs. The platypus and echidna are the only living monotremes.

Nucleus Central "core" of a complex cell.

Omnivore An animal that eats both plants and animals.

Palaeontologist A person who studies fossils.

Radioactivity A special form of energy which is given off during the breakdown, or decay, of certain chemical substances that are present in an unstable state.

Reptiles The scaly, land-living, backboned animals. Modern forms include turtles, lizards, snakes and crocodiles. The fossil forms include dinosaurs and pterosaurs.

Species A group of very similar plants and animals that are all closely related. All human beings are one species, while all dogs are another.

Vertebrate An animal with a backbone. Vertebrates are a large group that includes fish, amphibians, reptiles, birds and mammals.

INDEX

Photographic Credits:
Abbreviations: t-top m-middle
b-bottom l-left

Front cover m, 11, 17b: Bruce Coleman Ltd; Front cover b, 23t: Roger Vlitos; title p, 2t, 5b, 9, 16t, 17ml, 19m, 20b, 24t: Natural History Museum; 3t, 4, 5t, 7, 21b, 24b, 26 both, 27: Hulton Deutsch; 13, 28:Spectrum Colour Library; 15, 16b, 18, 19b:Science Photo Library; 17t, 20t, 21t, 23b: Mary Evans Picture Library; 17mr: Planet Earth Pictures; 19t: Ronald Grant Archive; 25: Eye Ubiquitous.